Inter-Faith

Worship?

by

Peter R. Akehurst
Vicar of Christ Church, Totland Bay, Isle of Wight

and

R. W. F. Wootton
Canon Emeritus of Lahore, Diocesan Chaplain for Community Relations, Leicester

GROVE BOOKS
BRAMCOTE NOTTS.

CONTENTS

FOREWORD

This is not the booklet either of us would have written alone. We hope the result is all the better for our collaboration. Obviously some parts are more the responsibility of one than the other—no prizes are offered for attempts at literary criticism. So far as possible we share general responsibility for what each has written, acknowledging that the other might have done it differently. We record our gratitude to the members of the Group for Renewal of Worship who have prodded us into this enterprise; at the same time we recognise how much we owe to many people over a wide area of grass roots experiment and discussion on the subject of Inter-Faith Worship. The material inevitably affects most closely the situation in Leicester, and we are aware it is not comprehensive in treating all individual religions, as, e.g. Judaism. Nevertheless, we hope the principles presented here will be of wide application.

P.R.A.
R.W.F.W.

First Impression July 1977

ISSN 0305 3067

ISBN 0 905422 16 3

1. THE CHANGING FACE OF BRITAIN

Life for Christians in Britain—as indeed for others—is a many-sided experience of pluralism. No one can be a long-term or short-term client of the National Health Service without being cared for at some level by people of another race and culture. One can only travel on London's public transport (below ground or above) because many who operate these services have immigrant community origins. The High Street shops (New Town or old) as a matter of course carry stranger names and scripts than the already familiar Chinese Restaurant. Quite apart from voluntary or contrived residence in cultural ghettos, life, at least in urban Britain, is a mixed if by no means thoroughly integrated experience.

The media reflect this state of affairs and bring it into our living rooms. Many schools prepare our children for it. Local urban government is influenced by it. It is a live issue in national politics. The churches are being jostled into facing it. There is a changing face to Britain today.

Similar forces of change affect church life. Mission is no longer allowable as something carried on elsewhere by those called 'foreign missionaries'. We now recognise that mission is one entire dimension of the Church universal's life. Many missionary societies are switching some of their resources of manpower and money from 'there' to 'here'; chaplains are appointed for immigrant communities, many of whom are former 'foreign' missionaries and much of their work is educative of domiciled native British congregations as well as serving the immigrant constituency. Redundant church buildings, sold or leased, are used by members of other faiths. Ministers from other countries and cultures are often to be found for longer or shorter periods helping congregations in Britain to fulfil their ministry and mission.

Changes, however, are not only to be found in the white British sector. Some of the world faiths are themselves resurgent and actively proselytizing in mission to the western world. The concepts of other faiths are being taken seriously in the west, particularly in relation to contemporary oriental spirituality and the Guru cults[1]. In an alien setting the practice of their faith takes on an added significance for immigrant populations as an important factor in the preservation of group identity. This may result both in more protective, self-conscious attitudes and in the emphasis of their distinctiveness due to a natural pride and the desire to be recognised as distinct, and accepted and esteemed in wider society. It may also result in a closing of the ranks to the outsider, out of fear of contamination by the godless society around.

Pew-level Pluralism

Perhaps we may personalize such generalizations by setting up a model of St. So-and-So's. In this urban parish we may meet Johnny in the Sunday School (or Family Service); he plays with Jamil at school and has just

---

[1] Well documented by Kenneth Leech in chapter 1 of *Soul Friend* (Sheldon Press, 1977).

heard about and been intrigued by the Divali Festival of Lights. In the Wives' Fellowship his mother, Bridget, through a casual chat at the local clinic has begun to help with a scheme to teach English to Asian women-folk in their homes. His father, Sam, is a sidesman; he works in the munici-pality's personnel department and finds himself involved with delicate negotiations about Sikhs wearing turbans at work. The organist (also a science teacher!) is a member of a Deanery Synod group involved with a pilot study of missionary giving and economic aid for poorer nations. Gail is a student who turns up in the vacations, enthusiastic about contriving mix-up experiences and religious cross-fertilization; she is an activist for demonstrations of solidarity in the face of injustice and would like to see other ways of worship and meditation experimented with in the local church.

Of course such fictitious characters will not all be found in any one parish but they serve without further elaboration to enable us to visualize pluralism as *the* contemporary context of Christian spirituality and mission today. To say this is not to deplore a reduction in Christian influence in society in triumphalist terms, for pluralism actually holds out to Christians new possibilities of learning from those of other faiths[1]. It makes instead a context for receiving as well as for giving. The practice of their religion, for example, by many Asians in Britain is of greater importance for them than it is for many a native Britisher.

These facts constitute a distinctive social experience for Christians in Britain. It is one which differs from that of the small Christian minority under a dominant non-Christian culture and philosophy such as is to be found in most parts of the non-western world. It also differs from that of the nominally Christian Britain containing a non-Christian minority which we had come to regard as the norm of western society up to the time of the Second World War. By contrast with each of these models we are now faced with an entirely newly experienced pluralism for Christians in Britain[2]. The implications of this for inter-faith worship are that the desider-ata of the earlier missionary or nominally Christian Britain situation cannot simply be transferred wholesale to the new situation. The new pluralism requires new standards and guidelines for inter-faith worship.

Pressures for common worship arise as a result of this situation and experi-ence[3]. In schools it influences the curriculum for the study of religion and the planning of school assemblies. In civic life it is felt in calls for the common keeping and celebration of United Nations Day, Commonwealth Day, Human Rights, World Peace and Justice Vigils, etc., and also from

[1] 'Pluralism in religion and culture provides an opportunity to learn and understand at first hand.' David Bronnert in *Obeying Christ in a Changing World,* Vol. 3 (Collins, 1977), p.130.

[2] Section II of a Report (1968) by a working group of the Faith and Order Department of the British Council of Churches deals with 'the new situation of religious pluralism in Britain'.

[3] The growing swell of pressure for all-faiths services is outlined in *Inter Faith Worship* ed. M. Braybrooke (Galliard, 1974).

time to time in local community affairs[1]. In the churches many feel that men of all faiths should stand together in a secularist age.

Before the movement for inter-faith worship attains the fantasy proportions of a religious Olympic Games march-past, each group bearing its flag of faith, to the accompaniment of anthems, liturgies and rituals as a preliminary to the real business of all-out competition for publicity and Gold Medals, this booklet seeks to raise issues of principle which need prior consideration. Recognising how easy it is for the church to jump on a contemporary bandwagon, we believe there are important issues of worship, theology and mission to be faced before occasions for common worship can rightly be set up. Our plea is that we relate to the theology of worship and mission as well as to the practicalities and expediencies of this new situation.

---

[1] The Silver Jubilee was one of these occasions and was observed in Leicester, among other places, by inter-community prayers. This is an example of an area where community and religion interact and overlap.

2. THE WORSHIP DIMENSION

Men of faith commonly do certain things as a result of or to express their faith. A sociological approach to religion identifies and examines these actions. They are recognizable as a distinct group of behavioural and role patterns which, though also found in other social contexts, are explicitly characteristic of religion. Worship is one of the major characteristic phenomena of religion. Religious people worship.

In worship the worshipper reaches out from himself towards the object worshipped. We may distinguish three basic modes:

1. *Word-centred worship;* this is bound up with reading, hearing, repeating sacred texts which may be classic resource documents or liturgies.

2. *Action-centred worship;* this is intended to appease or establish contact, union or relationship with the object of worship and may be effected by sacrifice or ritual patterns. These actions may be carried out by an acknowledged professional leader, by the whole group together, or by the individual worshipper.

3. *Thought-centred worship;* this is typically some form of group or individual meditation resulting in varying states of paranormal consciousness, involving growth in awareness and personal development.

Special techniques will be found in any of these modes of worship which cover posture, place, sound, song, smell, recitation, silence, meditation, ritual, the use of veneration of symbol or its absence. Modes of worship obviously overlap and are combined in varied mixtures in the worship experience of any one faith. Some of the techniques and modes are common to all faiths, some are peculiar to one faith, and some are more characteristic of one than another.

Worship and World-view
The meaning and purpose of worship depends on the world-view of the worshipper as developed in any particular religious faith. All who worship have in common at least a spiritual rather than materialistic understanding of reality. They recognise a spiritual dimension to life. Such a worshipful view of life is not an optional extra to be tacked on to other understandings of reality; it is a fundamental approach to human existence.

Within this general requirement of religion there are important differences in world-view between faiths. Animistic worship at one level often conceives the world as inhabited by many spirits able to exercise power over human lives; hence its task is to establish good relations with them, to propitiate them when angry by sacrifice and other rituals, and in general to manipulate them in accordance with the needs and concerns of the worshipper. Hindu worship may spring from the concept of monism, the unity of all existence, which denies transcendence and the distinction between Creator and creation. In that case worship will be seen as an aid to 'realising the divine within'. On the other hand (and this is more likely in Britain) it may be centred on one of the gods or *avatars* (incarnations), most probably Krishna, seen as a manifestation of God who is conceived to some extent in monotheistic terms. Such worship is normally performed before an idol and includes offerings to the god. Here the Hindu in his personal devotion (*bhakti*) to Krishna comes closest to Christian worship, yet the fact of idolatry, an inseparable part of temple worship, emphasises the difference and also removes from normality and a sense of reality any attempt at Hindu worship away from the shrine and in the presence of people of other faiths.

The three great monotheistic faiths have much in common in the area of worship because they share a world-view which centres on the transcendent God, the Creator and Judge of all men. To him their adherents offer the adoration which is his due and seek to conform their lives to his will. Yet here, too, the dogmatic differences between the faiths make united worship in a meaningful sense difficult. The norm of Muslim worship is the five statutory prayers decreed by Muhammad, the unique 'Apostle of God'. Many Muslim prayers, including that most frequently uttered, the Surat al Fatiha,[1] can be recited by Jew or Christian with a good conscience; but uttered in an Islamic context or in the presence of Muslims they take on a different meaning, hardly acceptable to those who do not recognise the authority of Muhammad. Thus in the Fatiha 'the straight highway' means to Muslims simply the way of Islam. The concept of Jesus as Saviour and Mediator, which underlies Christian prayer and worship even when it is not explicit, is a stumbling block to the other faiths, while to call God 'Father' is in Muslim eyes to detract from his transcendent glory.

'Common' worship should presuppose a degree of unanimity or at least a broadly overlapping framework or world-view, otherwise the common experience would be nonsense. There is, of course, a major division here between faith and unfaith. Men of different faiths will have more in common with one another than with men of no faith at all. On the basis, then, of the behavioural and relational patterns, the techniques and attitudes which are met with when men worship, it might be expected that a common, recognizable social phenomenon labelled 'worship' could be built up.

Many Faiths—One God?
This view, that on the basis of worship as a phenomenon of religion a valid common worship experience can be produced by drawing on all faiths, generally goes along with a particular world view held implicitly by many enthusiasts for inter-faith worship, though they may not fully acknowledge it.This is sometimes called 'syncretism'; but a more correct term, though not wholly satisfactory, is 'the equality of all religions'. That elusive and many-sided phenomenon, the Hindu religion, is on the whole undogmatic and is not based on a historical revelation. It is easy for the Hindu to say that there are many paths which all lead to God. In a sense he is obliged to say this, for his own faith-community contains many contradictions, such as that

[1] See p.20 below.

between the strictest *ahimsa* (harmlessness) and animal sacrifice, both practised by Hindus.

Some western scholars have appeared to adopt a similar approach. The latest exponent of such a view is Professor John Hick, of Birmingham University, who urges it with clarity and eloquence in his book *God and the Universe of Faiths* (Macmillan, 1973). Here Chapter 9 is entitled 'The Copernican Revolution in Theology'. He describes the various ways in which the old dogma of 'no salvation outside the Church' has been modified by Roman Catholic thinkers who still retain Christianity at the centre of the universe of faiths. Then he injects his new thesis: just as the Copernican revolution 'involved a shift from the dogma that the earth is the centre of the revolving universe to the realization that it is the sun that is the centre, with all the planets including our own earth revolving round it', so a theological revolution is needed, involving 'a shift from the dogma that Christianity is at the centre to the realization that it is God who is at the centre and that all the religions of mankind, including our own, serve and revolve around him.'

In the following chapters Hick develops his theory. First he treats it historically, tracing 'religion without revelation' in early cultures, then pointing to 'moments of divine revelation' from the time of Amos to the rise of Islam. The great religions are 'encounters from different historical and cultural standpoints with the same infinite divine reality', whether it is seen as personal or impersonal[1]. In chapters 11 and 12 he turns to the problem of how such an outlook can be squared with the Christian's devotion to Jesus. He expounds the difficulties in doctrines of the Incarnation, arguing that it 'lacks a content or meaning in virtue of which the statement that Jesus is God made man could be literally true or false'. He then asserts that the Incarnation is a myth, defining myth as a 'story which is not literally true . . . but which invites a particular attitude in its hearers', the myth being true if that attitude is appropriate[2]. He applies the same category to the Muslim teaching about the inspiration of the Qur'an and the claims made for Krishna in the Gita.

What are we to make of this? Clearly we are faced with a choice. We can either accept Hick's arguments and be content to recognise Christ as one of several revelations of God made to different nations and in different eras and equally valid, or we can affirm with the Bible and with Christians of all traditions, Orthodox, Catholic and Protestant, that Christ is utterly unique, differing from all other prophets and sages not in degree but in kind. Such an affirmation is the only one that does justice to the New Testament, whether we are thinking of Christ's own claims[3] or those made by his disciples[4]. As a consequence, any defence of inter-faith worship which is based on a world-view such as Hick's (and many advocates of such worship appear to be thinking along these lines, though they may not

[1] Hick *God and the Universe of Faiths* (Macmillan 1973),p.141.
[2] *op. cit.* pp.166-8.
[3] e.g. Matt. 11.27, 25.31f, 28.18f; Mark 14.62; John 8.58, 10.30, 14.6.
[4] e.g. Acts 4.12; Col. 1.15-19; Titus 2.13; Heb. 1.1-3; Rev. 22.13.

realize it) presents grave difficulties to many Christians, and they will be very reluctant to engage in it if by so doing they seem to be countenancing such a view.

A Distinct Dimension

The Christian world-view gives a distinctiveness, not to say, exclusiveness, to Christian worship—'Christian worship is not simply a channel of religious feeling or an inroad to the mystery of God. It is an approach by thinking men to a God about whom beliefs are held . . .'[1] Without attempting to elaborate a thorough-going theology of worship we suggest that distinctively Christian worship is:

1. *Responsive worship;* God's action comes first and man responds to this. It is not man's initiative in reaching out or up, down or within, to God but man's response to God's prior reach to him[2].

2. *Salvation-centred worship;* it arises out of God's meeting of man's need and so Christian worship is more than merely creaturely worship in the presence of the Creator-spirit; it is the redeemed worship of man in the presence (and experience) of a saving God.

3. *Corporate in context;* it is done with others in a body, *the Body of Christ,* the worship of the redeemed community with a mission in the world. It will therefore spill over into matters of mutual relationship within the worshipping community and responsible ethical stewardship of the material world itself[3].

Christian worship, therefore, will be geared to a particular kind of penitence, faith, surrender, adoration, communion, obedience and service which will be distinguishable from the same worship-attitudes expressed in the worship of other faiths.

Though a neutral technique, set of roles and behaviour pattern may be apparent in the worship of all faiths, Christianity adds to this a specific and unique theological content. When inter-faith worship is mooted it must be asked whether men of different faiths are doing intrinsically the same thing when they worship, or whether it is a case of separate and different things being done side by side. We believe that the distinctiveness of worship on any count—whether Muslim, Jewish or Christian—is such that it cannot easily be engaged in together and that if this is to be attempted

---

[1] J. L. Houlden in *The Eucharist Today—Studies on Series 3,* ed. R. C. D. Jasper (SPCK 1974), p.175.

[2] 'Perhaps the most adequate single word to do justice to the paradox of worship is the word "response" . . . Worship is our response to what God reveals to us of himself.' Michael Perry *The Paradox of Worship* (SPCK, 1977) p.19.

[3] 'A service of worship presupposes commitment. The worshippers are not . . . necessarily committed to a particular and dogmatic corpus of beliefs, but they *are* committed to a body of people which is the heir to and trustee of those beliefs. They are also, if the worship is Christian worship, committed to a Person who is the truth . . .' (author's italics). Perry *op. cit* p.31.

very clear guidelines and safeguards need to be set out[1]. By contrast, some examples of inter-faith worship appear almost to be a conscious attempt to blur theological exactitude, so asking people to say what they do not and cannot mean. This is to be deplored.

We do not think it too far-fetched to question if 'worship' is the right word to be applied to inter-faith worship! A common religious activity could have value. It will certainly not necessarily be worship in the Christian sense. Equally, it might not rate as worship in an Islamic or Jewish sense. Perhaps, after all, we need some other word to describe the common awareness or response men of all faiths could make together

In this context it is pertinent to criticize a 'Call to Worship' issued by the Cambridge Branch of the United Nations Association, 1975. It declares 'We have come together to think of those things that lie nearest to our hearts, to dwell on those ideals towards which we are aiming, to acknowledge the vision that has come to us in moments of truth.' It goes on to say 'Let us unite in our endeavour to cast off all that separates us from each other; may we learn to respect one another; and to know the presence of that Spirit which unites us all.' This is a valid enough activity in its own right, but to what extent can Christians call it worship?

More attention to a sociological approach to worship, centred in the action and roles of worshipping, might provide a useful way forward. Our plea is for a deliberately low profile worship, not a debased coin—for worship based in a creaturely, behavioural stance, exploring techniques of worship together, affirming values together, and engaging in the silence of listening and meditation together. Such 'religious P.T.' or flexing of religious muscles together could remove both the need for triumphalism, the feeling of being threatened, and the belief that worship had been evacuated of all meaning. It could validly be done in the context of modern pluralistic society. If it is theologically too threatening and unsatisfying to piece together a mosaic of bits from the classic sacred texts of the world's faiths and liturgies, less pretence may be involved in setting limited aims of this nature.

[1] The BCC Faith and Order Dept. Report (Braybrooke *op. cit.* pp.5-6) refers to difficulties arising 'from the conception of worshipping together in a sense which implies that the whole gathered congregation participates equally in the whole service. . . . The way forward would seem to be (a) opportunities for Christians to exchange visits with those of other faiths for sympathetic and instructed observation of another's worship (b) occasions on which those of different faiths do in turn what is characteristic of their own religion, enabling others present to share to the extent to which they conscientiously can. The concept will thus be each religious community doing its worship in the same place, but not worshipping together in the sense of claiming to share in the same act of worship.'

3. THE MISSIONARY DIMENSION

The traditional attitude of Christian missionaries to other faiths has been one of hostility, and at times it has gone as far as to attribute their origin to Satan's influence, with some support from St. Paul's attitude to Graeco-Roman religion[1]. But Paul himself was glad to draw support from the thinking about God of some Greek philosophers, especially the Stoics,[2] and Gregory the Great urged that even heathen temples and festivals should be taken over for Christian use and as it were 'baptized into Christ'. So today many evangelists working among those of other faiths seek to find points of contact in them, to adopt a positive attitude to them wherever possible and to welcome all that is good and true in them. Where the other faith commands the allegiance of the majority, this positive attitude has very rarely reached the point of accepting joint worship, but no doubt this is because Christians feel themselves on the defensive in this situation and are fearful of being overwhelmed or absorbed; there is also concern about the possible effect of such action on new converts or potential converts.

Where, however, Christianity is the historic faith, no such consideration inhibits Christians. Many of them naturally desire to build all possible bridges across the gap which divides the races as in many British cities today. This involves in the first place working for social justice for all and seeking friendly relationships between individuals and groups. The next step is trying to establish contact on a cultural level by encouraging appreciation of the culture of minority groups through (for instance) participation in music and dance together, through the discussion of differing attitudes to family life, the generation gap, and so on. Since Asian attitudes to such topics are closely tied up with religion, it is but a short step to sharing views and feelings on that level too. Indeed without this there can be no proper understanding of cultural differences.

Then when the Christian participant is surprised to find that many of his ideas of other faiths are apparently mistaken, and that he has a good deal in common with them as presented by their adherents (who may, of course, be selective and make subtle adjustments to suit a Christian audience), he naturally thinks, 'These people are my fellow men, bound up with me in the bundle of life. They too believe in God. Their faith means much to them; their life has a spiritual dimension far more truly than that of the mass of people around. Why should we not take our stand together as men of faith in a world of unbelief? Why should we not name the name of God together in love and truth? Why should we not show that religion is a uniting, rather than a divisive, force by publicly worshipping together?'

Common Humanity—Unique Redemption

Clearly such an attitude cannot be dismissed out of hand. It springs from a deep sense of a common humanity, of a relationship of mutual understanding and trust in sharp contrast with the prejudice and indifference

[1] 1 Cor. 10.20.
[2] Acts 17.22-31.

11

sometimes exploding into hatred, which is seen around. Many Christians have come to feel that the values seen in Asian communities are in some ways superior to those of secular society around, and therefore Asians should be helped to preserve their cultural identity and the religion on which it is based; the alternative seems to be a slide into secularism and loss of identity, which has already been seen to be harmful in the case of young Asians who have rebelled against the restrictions of traditional family life and have sometimes drifted into drink, drugs or prostitution. Inter-faith worship is seen as a means to counteract such a slide, as it assures newcomers that their religion is respected and indeed encouraged by the majority community. But the impression is also given that Christians no longer desire to make conversions from other faiths, and this is indeed the attitude of most of those who advocate inter-faith worship.

Others would urge that the Great Commission to make disciples, though uttered in a completely different situation, is valid for all time and that the Christian in loyalty to Christ has no right to withhold the saving message of the Gospel from his neighbours, whatever their faith. They feel that the risk involved in uprooting someone from his own faith-community through conversion does not invalidate the Lord's command, and that the Christian must balance that command with his respect for other faiths and his desire for the all-round welfare of his neighbours, who should be allowed to live their lives with freedom and dignity and to follow the religion and culture of their choice. A clergyman, formerly a missionary, finds no real conflict between these demands, though they may certainly compete for priority. Thus when visiting Asian prisoners in the local jail, he passes on to them scriptures and other Christian books in the appropriate languages, but when asked by a Sikh prisoner for a prayer book of his own faith he was glad to supply it. In the same way he often takes Christians to the Hindu temple, where Hindu faith and worship are explained to them, and if a group of Muslims needed a place for a mosque he would help them to obtain it. At the same time he seeks opportunities to speak of Christ to people of other faiths and sometimes sets up a table stocked with Christian books in several languages in the park to sell them to the Asian people who frequent it.

Witness by Dialogue

Many people in this situation find other opportunities than inter-faith worship of showing their sense of human brotherhood and their respect and concern for those of other faiths. On the directly religious level the way of dialogue (to use a convenient, though overused, term) is open to them. They can sit down with friends of another faith to share together the riches which each has found in his own faith. For the Christian this will involve listening with real attention to what the other person has to say and welcoming all that there is of truth and goodness which his friend has found. He may even be challenged in his own faith as he sees truths which he has not so far apprehended or perhaps has long ago forgotten. All truth is God's truth, and he need have no fear in entering into such an exercise. Then when the time comes he will have the privilege of sharing the un-fathomable riches of Christ in a gracious and humble way with the other person. To regard such an exercise as a subtle form of evangelism would be dishonest, for that is not its purpose. But it may certainly have the effect of preparing the way for the Gospel, as well as giving the Christian a new insight into the other faith. Such occasions of dialogue may also be more formally structured ,with speakers on a particular topic, such as 'knowing God', 'finding peace', 'the purpose of life', followed by open questions and then by discussion in small groups; the last phase is generally the most profitable, as it involves personal meeting.

Many feel that dialogue of this kind is most desirable, but are unwilling to take the further step of going on to joint worship, because they feel that would compromise their loyalty to Christ, and if they are in touch with Christian converts and wish to see people turn to Christ from other faiths, they feel that inter-faith worship would be a serious obstacle in the way. Others, however, have found that the situation of dialogue itself has led on naturally to the offering up to God together of the concerns, the hopes and the aspirations which they and their friends have come to share in the course of the dialogue. This raises the question of appropriateness which we shall consider in the next chapter.

4. THE PRACTICAL DIMENSION

We pass now to a consideration of how, when, and where common worship may arise. Hardly overt worship, but worthy of notice is the use of buildings—selling or lending redundant buildings and helping to provide suitable places for worship for men of other faiths.

People of other faiths are faced with real difficulties in seeking to carry out the corporate obligations of their faith in Britain. While the Muslim can offer his prayers in any clean place, there is an obligation to pray together at least every Friday and on festival days. Corporate worship where the *Granth Sahib* is read and the praises of God are sung together is very important for Sikhs. Hindu worship normally involves offerings made before the images of the gods in a place dedicated for this purpose. Further, to have a rallying point for the community in a society where it forms a small minority is obviously important for any group.

Buildings and Worship

In the inner city where most people of other faiths live there is rarely any space where new worship centres can be erected, and the cost of so doing is generally prohibitive. In the same areas there are often unused church properties, and it is natural that they should look to them as possible places for their worship. Whatever Christians may feel about the rightness of sharing their place of worship with people of other faiths, this is generally out of the question because of the especial accoutrements and arrangements which are required, while the presence of Christian symbols and fixed chairs or pews may present difficulties for their worship. But church halls are hired out from time to time for weddings of other faiths and for cultural activities, religious dance and drama etc., which go with Hindu festivals. To do so seems to be an act of goodwill on the part of Christians, who wish to see the newcomers live their lives with freedom and dignity in the way to which they are accustomed.

These questions were examined carefully by a working party of the British Council of Churches (sitting 1972-74)[1], and their recommendations included the following:

> 'Church premises other than areas devoted to regular Christian worship should be made available to those of other Faiths for their social purposes. Those who can do so conscientiously, legally and with pastoral responsibility should also make such premises available to people of other Faiths for their religious purposes.'

But the recommendation of the Interim Report of the same group that

> 'Premises which, having been used for regular Christian worship, are declared redundant and stripped of Christian symbols, should be made available on appropriate terms to those of other Faiths for any purpose for which they may require . . .'

[1] *The Community Orientation of the Church* (BCC, 1974) pp.14, 17-18. The whole report deserves study.

met with considerable opposition and could only be commended for further study. In fact a number of redundant churches of various denominations have been converted into centres of other-faith worship.

Common Worship in Schools

The whole question of inter-faith worship in multi-faith schools is a difficult one as is that of religious education itself. Without entering into these important issues it should generally be agreed that children growing up in a multi-racial society ought to know something about the faiths of their neighbours, and therefore it is appropriate that at Hindu festivals, for example, dance, drama and readings connected with them should be presented by the Hindu children before the whole school, just as a nativity play will probably be shown at Christmas. One danger is that all such spectacles may be consigned in the minds of the children to the 'fairy story' category, but this danger is present even in schools where no other faith but the Christian is recognised. Care, however, needs to be taken, e.g., in regard to any act of worship which might form part of the presentation, and if this is to be Hindu worship then only Hindu children should participate. Further the consciences of Christian teachers who are asked to prepare such an event must be respected, should they feel unable to do so.

But perhaps the greatest danger in multi-faith schools is of giving the impression that all religions are not only worthy of respect but are also of equal validity, and some songs commonly used would seem to imply this. Indeed it is hard to see how a religious assembly can take place regularly for children of different faiths in an atmosphere of mutual respect without this implication being given. No doubt social, creational and theistic topics, the needs of the suffering, the practice of loving concern etc. can occupy much of the time, but without going beyond these subjects justice cannot really be done to any of the religions concerned. This is an important topic which deserves a book on its own.

Visiting Other Worshipping Groups

One way by which Christians and those of other faiths can get to know each other and appreciate each other's culture is by visiting their places of worship and observing acts of corporate worship. In general this is welcomed by the hosts though the situation differs radically from one religion to another, and a Christian wishing to arrange such a visit needs to go about it with some care. Muslims will generally welcome visitors to a mosque and explain the principles of Islam to them. On occasions, too, they may be happy for Christians to sit or stand by reverently while they perform their prayer ritual; this will not however normally be possible at the congregational service on a Friday as there will not be room. When arranging such a visit it should be clarified beforehand whether the Muslim hosts expect women to be in the party, as Muslim women do not normally pray in a mosque with the men. It will be difficult to arrange an official return visit to a church, though individual Muslims of more liberal views may perhaps accept an invitation.

With regard to the Hindus, a similar visit will most certainly be welcomed during the time of the evening worship of the gods (generally about

6.30 p.m.) and the period of singing and reading which follows it. At the end a Hindu leader will explain the images and pictures, the meaning of the ceremonies and so on. He will also be pleased to feel that the visitors are in some sense joining in the worship (this would be implied if a visitor followed the example of the worshippers and bowed with joined hands before the images), so a Christian would wish to make clear his position as an observer and not a participator. As he is leaving he will be offered something to eat—a fruit or sweetmeat generally—which has in fact been offered to the god, a practice which brings 1 Corinthians 8.10 right up to date. Groups of Hindus will often respond to an invitation to visit a church service on a special occasion, and will be happy to stay for tea and biscuits etc. afterwards. Christian books, such as the gospels in appropriate languages, may be offered to them.

Worship in the *gurdwara* (Sikh temple) is free from idolatry, so the same problems do not arise. Christians are warmly welcomed to the main service of the week (about noon on Sunday). They will take off their shoes (as in mosque and Hindu temple) and cover their heads—cloths are generally provided for the purpose. They may sit down in the congregation (without doing obeisance to the sacred book, as the Sikhs do) and listen to the singing, reading and exhortation—in Panjabi of course! Sometimes Christians are even given the opportunity of speaking to the congregation. The service generally takes two hours or more, but none will be offended if one arrives late or leaves early. It is followed by a meal to which they will be welcomed.

Christians need have no qualms about this kind of religious inter-change. It is interpreted by Asian people as expressive of friendliness and respect. It helps them to find their place in our society, if they feel that the majority community is interested in their culture and religion (the two are inextricably bound together) and regards them as worthy of observation and study. In explaining their faith Hindus and Sikhs will often make statements about the basic unity of all religions—'Different ways to the same God' or 'We all worship the same God by different names'—and the Christian may well feel that he must prevent misunderstanding by courteously expressing his dissent from his outlook.

Avowed Multi-faith Worship

A different situation arises where people of two or more faiths meet together on neutral ground and engage in acts of worship. A conference of Christians and Muslims may begin with a recitation of the Qur'an in Arabic followed by translation and by a reading from the Bible. Each group listens with respect to the other's scripture, and no particular problem arises. If however later in the conference a careful selection of Muslim and Christian prayers is read by one person, or people are invited at the same time to offer petitions arising out of the concern which they have shared together during their meeting, the position is somewhat different. Such acts may be felt as a natural expression of the mutual respect and understanding the conference has generated, and therefore altogether appropriate.

16

On occasions too, more elaborate services have been devised for people of different faiths living together in a particular place or perhaps sharing a holiday together, services which have included readings, songs and prayers. Here however an element of unreality is almost bound to creep in. Christian hymns are 'expurgated', i.e., references to Jesus or to specifically Christian concepts are omitted; or again elements remain which are not really meaningful or acceptable to the person of another faith, e.g., references to the atonement in several services we have examined. It is extremely difficult to devise an acceptable service of this kind.

In 1966 considerable controversy arose over a service at St. Martin's-in-the-Fields, London, in the presence of Her Majesty the Queen, in which Christians, Hindus, Muslims and Buddhists took part. This involved four affirmations, readings from various scriptures, a hymn ('All people that on earth do dwell') and a series of blessings. The occasion was Commonwealth Day, so the political purpose was clear enough, and the element of personal knowledge and appreciation between the participants was lacking. The service aroused considerable opposition, mainly because it was felt to give official support at a high level to the 'equality of all religions'. The Convocation of Canterbury passed a resolution 'viewing with concern the holding of multi-religious services in Christian Churches', and later the Secretaries of Anglican Missionary Societies issued a statement concluding, 'while true dialogue between Christians and adherents of other religions is to be encouraged, local churches should be strongly advised not to provide for inter-faith services.'

Following this the British Council of Churches gave close attention to the matter, and the report of an *ad hoc* group appointed for the purpose was received by the Council in April 1968 with appreciation. This report encouraged the exchange of visits with those of other faiths for 'sympathetic and instructed observation of each other's worship' and also 'occasions on which those of different faiths did in turn what is characteristic of their own religion, enabling the others present to share to the extent to which they conscientiously can'. At the same time it warned in the strongest terms against 'anything which may suggest that Jesus Christ is one of many saviours'.

Most Christian churches have followed the guide lines laid down. However a Multi-Faith Act of Witness for the Commonwealth, similar to that held in St. Martin's-in-the-Fields in 1966, has continued to be observed in the Guildhall of London annually with Christian participators. Further the World Congress of Faiths is wholeheartedly committed to inter-faith worship, and at its annual conference an explicit 'All-Faiths Service' is held, in which people from seven faiths participate. In this most space is given to readings from the various scriptures; there is also an address and prayers are offered. There are several hymns, all of Christian origin, but sometimes considerably adapted; e.g. John Oxenham's 'In Christ there is no east or west' becomes 'In God there is no east or west'—one wonders what the author's reaction would have been to this. While there is much in these services which is true and inspiring, many Christians would feel out of place in them, as their whole trend is to minimise the difference between the faiths. In one of them (that of 1970) the only reference to Christ in the printed service is in a Hindu's prayer, linking him with Shiva, Buddha and others as names under which the Lord of the Universe is worshipped. Many would feel that to take a full part in such a service would seriously compromise their loyalty to truth.

5. RESOURCE MATERIAL FOR INTER-FAITH WORSHIP

To a great extent one gathers one's own resources of ministry in a fairly personal way as one goes along. In this chapter we do no more than consider some of the resource material that has come our way, without any pretence at comprehensiveness.

Inter-Faith Worship (Ed. Marcus Braybrooke. Galliard, 1974. 60p) is the report of a working party of clergymen of the Church of England, Free Church and Roman Catholic Church, under the chairmanship of Edward Carpenter, President of the World Congress of Faiths. It calls attention to the mood of wider religious ecumenism evidenced in the Second Vatican Council, World Council of Churches' 'Dialogue with Men of Other Faiths and Ideologies', and the work of the World Congress of Faiths, and notes the development of inter-faith worship in India, Britain, America, the West Indies, Japan and Holland. As 'people of different faiths are being drawn together and discovering a unity in the service of man and in the search for and response to Eternal Truth' a basic distinction is drawn between acts of worship of one religious community incorporating material from another, and acts of worship intended to be deliberately inter-faith. It lists arguments in favour and arguments against inter-faith worship, and the views of other religions so far as they had been received by the working group are reported. A conclusion recognises that 'often the most fruitful way forward is for people of one religion to attend the worship of another religion' and recommends that such visits should be occasional, carefully planned, and with prior explanation. It also recognises that there are situations which call for joint worship and gives two examples of such worship as appendices.

These include: a Rig Veda prayer, suitable for an opening prayer (p.15): 'O God, let us be united . . .'; a prayer of personal dedication by Sir Jogendra Singh (p.19): 'O Lord, give me a heart . . .'; a Hebrew prayer of blessing the Creator (p.21): 'Blessed art thou, . . . King of the Universe, . . .'; a Hindu prayer of praise and supplication (p.21): 'We praise thee with our thoughts, O God . . .'

A third appendix lists suitable hymns which express praise to God and man's yearning for peace and unity, rather than 'watered-down' Christian hymns. A Bibliography covers inter-faith worship (mostly articles), school assemblies, and aids for those arranging inter-faith worship (collections of materials from the sacred scriptures and prayers of The World Religions).

Books dealing with general attitudes and relationships with people of other faiths are: *A New Threshold:* Guidelines for the Churches in their relations with Muslim communities (David Brown, BCC 50p) will repay study. A short chapter underlines the need for Christian response to Muslim communities to arise out of prayer and to be sustained by it. Two Islamic prayers are printed and mention is made of *Alive to God*, a selection of Christian and Muslim prayers on kindred themes, with a full introduction, (Kenneth Cragg, OUP £1·50) and *Muslim Devotions* (Constance Padwick, SPCK £3·95) as useful resources. *Doorways and Doorsteps* (David Brown,

CMS 15p) and *Living the Gospel* (David Bronnert, CMS 15p) pursue aspects of the individual and the Christian community's attitudes and relationship with men of other faiths. *Uncharted Journey* (Roger Hooker. CMS 20p) explores Hindu, Muslim and Christian devotion. It stretches us to think with men of other faiths—about their faith and ours.

Specific collections of prayers which might prove useful are:

The Prayers of African Religion (John S. Mbiti, SPCK £2·50) begins with a 22-page investigation of African spirituality. It then gathers prayers from Christian and other sources, grouping them under subject headings such as: prayers for the day, month, year; life, health and healing; wealth and prosperity; man's work; war and adversity; life's journey; the spirits; rain; offerings, sacrifices and dedications; confidence, confession and creed; praise, joy and thanksgiving; condemnation, blessings and peace.

Morning, Noon and Night (John Carden, CMS 25p) is a collection of Christian prayers and meditations from the Third World. They come from India, Japan, Africa and Persia.

One Man's Prayers (George Appleton, SPCK £1·25) contains a presentation of the Buddhist *Divine Exercises* in a form which can be used within 'a framework of my belief in God-in-Christ' (pp.80-83). Appleton also includes the Buddhist prayer or aspiration:

> Now may every living thing, young or old,
> weak or strong, living near or far, known
> or unknown, living or departed or yet unborn,
> may every living thing be full of bliss.

Religion in the Multi-Faith School (ed. W. Owen Cole. Yorks. Council for Community Relations, Hunslet Road, Leeds, 10). A very useful collection of many kinds of materials together with guidance for teachers.

With One Voice (ed. Sid G. Hedges, Religious Education Press, 1970). A collection of prayers and thoughts from world religions, designed for the multi-faith school, but useful for other occasions too.

Many *Psalms* are useful as common expressions of worship and dependence on God, and can be used by people of other faiths.

The following sacred texts may also prove of use:

An ancient Hindu hymn
> From the unreal lead me to the Real.
> From darkness lead me to light.
> From death lead me to immortality.

Surat al Fatiha (The first chapter of the Qur'an)
> In the name of the most Merciful and Compassionate God.
> Praise be to God, the Lord of the worlds, the most Merciful, the
> Compassionate, the Master of the day of judgment. Thee alone do

we worship and of thee alone do we beg assistance. Guide us in the right way, in the way of those to whom thou hast been gracious; not of those who have incurred wrath, nor of those who go astray.

Prayer of Rabiah (A Muslim woman mystic)

O my Lord, if I worship thee from fear of hell, burn me in hell; if I worship thee from hope of Paradise, shut me out from Paradise. But if I worship thee for thine own sake, then withhold not from me thine eternal beauty.

The Mul Mantra (Sikh daily prayer)

There is One God.
He is the Supreme Truth.
He, the creator,
Is without fear and without hate.
He, the Omnipresent,
Pervades the universe.
He is not born,
Nor does he die to be born again.
By his grace shalt thou worship him.
Before time itself
There was truth.
When time began to run its course
He was the truth.
Even now, he is the truth
And evermore shall truth prevail.

6. CONCLUSION

One of us finds himself moved primarily by his understanding and experience of mission and truth. He therefore rejects amalgams of watered-down truth and the possibility of a world-faith, as lacking in integrity and not basically satisfying to man's religious experience.

One of us finds himself moved primarily by his understanding and experience of worship. On the one hand he rejects liturgical mosaics composed of a piece here and a piece there gathered from the world's religions; on the other hand he rejects the calling of valid humanist affirmations 'worship'.

Both of us would say, if you are to have anything approaching inter-faith worship, here are some guidelines:

1. *It is best set to limited aims*
   These may be no more than the sharing of insights, the demonstration of religious postures and movements, the expression of a common creaturely response before the Creator.

2. *They must be based on mutual respect*
   This will start, at least, with an express desire for understanding, which may be shown in acknowledgment of one another's classic resources of faith, with recognition of the extent and limits of unity and the avoidance of threatening evangelism.

3. *They should grow out of prior relationship*
   Belonging together in some shared community, regional or locality life, common concern for justice, or shared study and search for meaning, may be the soil from which worship can spring and without which it remains unearthed in mutual relationship.

4. *They must avoid theological inconsistency*
   For the Christian there must be no implicit denial of the basic claims of Christ—he is Lord of all. As the British Council of Churches resolved in 1968 'Churches should scrupulously avoid those forms of inter-faith worship which compromise the distinctive faiths of the participants and should ensure that Christian witness is neither distorted nor muted.'

5. *They must avoid situational dishonesty*
   This would be deliberate ambiguity or blurring of meaning; making people say what they do not and cannot believe; and worship which does not issue in on-going commitment in concern, care and support.

We believe worship within these guidelines would be for the glory of God and the service of man.

GROVE LITURGICAL STUDIES (32 pages—**75p**) This series began in March 1975, and replaces the monthly booklet on Ministry and Worship every third month. The Studies are designed to be weightier, whilst still within the range of interest of non-specialists and students.

For Ministry and Worship titles see outside back cover. For others send for catalogue.

PERSONAL **ORDER SLIP** to GROVE BOOKS, BRAMCOTE, NOTTS. Please send the following on Standing Order (I will pay when I receive the invoice after six months with option of renewing):

................copies Ministry and Worship booklets beginning with no. ....

.... copies Liturgical Studies beginning with no. ....

.... copies Ethics booklets beginning with no. ....

.... copies *News of Liturgy* beginning from (month) 1977

The following (for which I enclose £................ and SAE):

....

....

....

....

Name...

Address ....

....

Please delete lines inapplicable